IN FOCUS: NATIVE AMERICANS

# DELAWARE

## HISTORY AND CULTURE



MARK STEWART

Cavendish Square

Published in 2026 by Cavendish Square Publishing, LLC
2544 Clinton Street, Buffalo, NY 14224



Website: cavendishsq.com



Portions of this work were originally authored by Joseph Stanley and published as *Delaware (Lenape)* (Spotlight on Native Americans). All new material this edition authored by Mark Stewart.



Publisher: Katie Kawa
Book Design: Lisa Miley

Portions of this work were reviewed by: Donald A. Grinde, Jr., Professor of Transnational/American Studies at the State University of New York at Buffalo.

Photo Credits: Anton Foltin/Shutterstock.com (4); Thomas McKenney/U.S. Department of War (5*); Author's Collection (6 top*, 19*); Songquan Deng/Shutterstock.com (6 bottom); John Hall (7*); Benjamin West (9*); George Catlin/National Gallery of Art (10*, 11*); Alfred Bobbett/Library of Congress (12*); Harper's New Monthly (13*); Chicago History Museum/Archive Photos/Getty Images (15); Thomas Campanius Holm/Historical Society of Pennsylvania (16*); MyLoupe/Universal Images Group/Getty Images (17); National Anthropological Archives (18*); Project Gutenberg (21*); Melissa McDermott/www.flickr.com/photos/melissamcdermott/15129036938 and 15128873509/CC BY-NC 2.0 (22, 26–27); Courtesy of the Brooklyn Public Library (23); Kansas Historical Society (25*); Lisa G/www.flickr.com/photos/emereyscape/1348443571/CC BY-NC-ND 2.0 (28); Columbia Undergraduate Admissions (29).

Cover images (clockwise from top): Benjamin West*; Melissa McDermott (see link above); National Anthropological Archives*; Henry Chapman Mercer*; George Catlin/National Gallery of Art*; Melissa McDermott/flickr.com (see links above).

*These images are in the public domain.

Cataloging-in-Publication Data
Names: Stewart, Mark, 1960 July 7-.
Title: Delaware history and culture / Mark Stewart.
Description: Buffalo, NY : Cavendish Square Publishing, 2026. | Series: In focus: Native Americans | Includes glossary and index.
Identifiers: ISBN 9781502674791 (pbk.) | ISBN 9781502674807 (library bound) | ISBN 9781502674814 (ebook)
Subjects: LCSH: Delaware Indians--Juvenile literature. | Delaware Indians--History--Juvenile literature. | Delaware Indians--Social life and customs--Juvenile literature.
Classification: LCC E99.D2 S94 2026 | DDC 974.004'97345--dc23

CPSIA compliance information: Batch #CS26CSQ: For further information contact Cavendish Square Publishing LLC at 1-877-980-4450.
Printed in the United States of America

# CONTENTS



**ABOUT OUR GLOSSARY**

In this book, there may be several words or terms you are reading for the first time, or words that are familiar but used in an unusual way. All of these words appear in **bold type** throughout the book and are defined on page 30.

# I AM THE LAND

The land surrounding the Hudson and Delaware Rivers in New Jersey and Southern New York is home to millions of people. The fertile valleys, thick forests, and **abundant** waters that drew the first European settlers there were once the **domain** of the Delaware people. The same settlers who named the Delaware River after Lord De La Ware—leader of the English settlement in Virginia—called the Native people who used the river as their main waterway the "Delaware Indians."

They called themselves the *Lenape* (meaning "original people") and the river *Lenapewihituk* (meaning

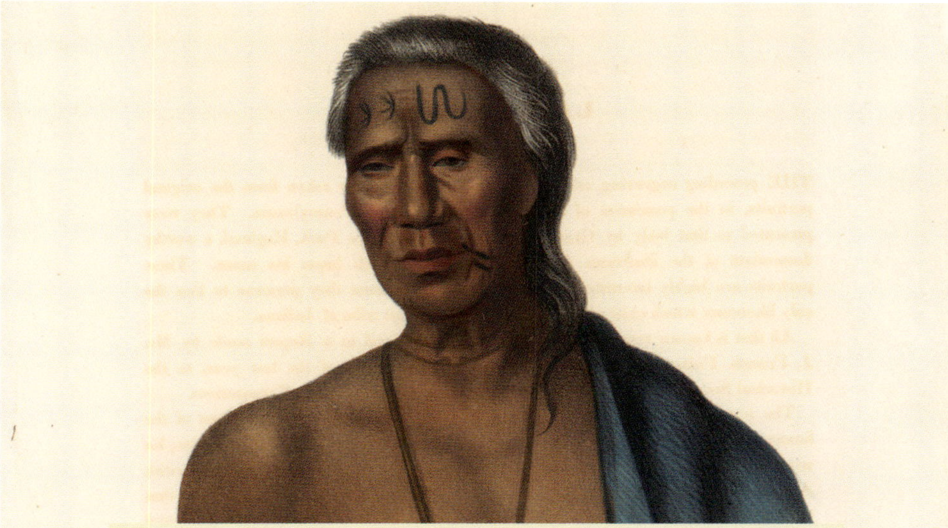

Lappawinsoe, a Lenape chief from the late 1600s, may have been the first Native American to have his portrait painted.

"river of the Lenape"). Other tribes sometimes referred to the Lenape as "grandfathers" because they had lived in the region so long.

The Lenape were an **Algonquian**-speaking tribe whose territory also included parts of Delaware, Pennsylvania, and Long Island, New York. They moved through their lands with the seasons, often coming together in large groups on the Atlantic seashore in the summer to hunt, fish, and grow crops. They understood

◀ The Lenape people used the Delaware River the way we use highways today.

The Lenape people acquired firearms from European settlers near the end of the 1600s.

their environment and lived in harmony with the natural world. The Lenape also were known as peacekeepers. Their leaders were often asked to help neighboring tribes to help settle disputes.

The Lenape were divided into three smaller groups. These groups were separated by where they lived and the **dialect** of the Lenape language they spoke. The Munsee people generally lived in the northern parts of the Lenape homelands. The Unami people lived in the central areas of Lenape land. The Unalachtigo people lived south of the Unami.

Wisdom and insight helped the Lenape search for solutions instead of inviting conflict. They were known by American colonists as "friendly" because they were willing to make agreements before taking up arms. With the arrival of more and more settlers, however, the Lenape were pushed ever westward—first into Pennsylvania and Ohio, and then across the Mississippi River. Some relocated to the Upper Midwest and Canada. Others remained in their ancestral lands. Wherever they went, the Lenape held on to their traditions and culture while finding ways to blend into other tribes.

◀ The Lenape were pushed ever westward from their beloved Delaware River in the 1700s.

In recent years, evidence has emerged of human presence in North America much earlier than previously thought—perhaps as long as 30,000 years ago. The northern ice sheet would have been impenetrable at that time, meaning that these people would have arrived by sea. Were the Lenape descendants of these early arrivals? Genetic research may one day provide an answer.

# FIRST CONTACT

The first group of settlers with whom the Lenape had regular contact were the Dutch. They used **commerce** to become a world power in the 1500s and controlled trade with Europe in the region where the Lenape lived. In 1626, the Dutch made an agreement with Munsee leaders to occupy the island of Manhattan in current-day New York City. The two cultures had very different understandings of what this deal meant. While the Munsee understood it as permission to use the land, the Dutch considered it a purchase—and the Lenape never again possessed this territory.

In 1682, the Lenape people west of the Delaware River came into contact with a group of English settlers led by William Penn. Penn respected the Lenape and pursued a friendly relationship. He agreed to purchase the land he needed to establish the colony of Pennsylvania, rather than taking it in the name of the king. Penn's sons, Thomas and John, did not deal as fairly with

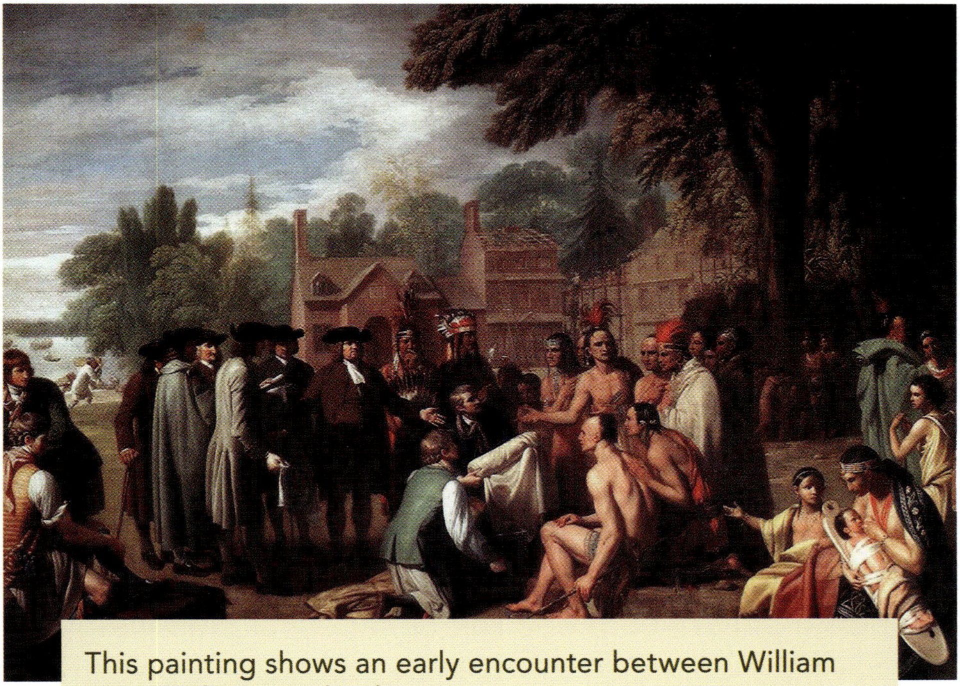

This painting shows an early encounter between William Penn and Lenape leaders.

the Lenape. In 1737, they claimed to have found a treaty from 1686 that granted as much land as a man could walk in one-and-a-half days. The brothers picked three of their fastest men and offered a prize to the one who covered the greatest distance. The Lenape, whose population already had been reduced from more than 20,000 to fewer than 5,000, lost an enormous amount of their remaining land in what came to be called the Walking Purchase.

# I AM A WARRIOR

For many centuries, Lenape boys and young men were trained as hunters and warriors with a bow and arrow. They went into battle with a knife, which was carried around the neck in a decorated sheath, along with a war club or tomahawk tucked into a belt or sash, which was also highly decorated. The Lenape war club weighed two to three pounds and was made of hardwood, with a thick head that often included a metal or stone blade. As Dutch settlers moved into Lenape territory in the 1600s, violence sometimes erupted. After the English **wrested** control from the Dutch in 1644, periodic conflict continued.

Lenape warriors did not fare well in these battles against more powerful European weapons. They began to trade

◀ Ni-co-man, a Lenape chief, is shown with his bow and arrows in a painting from the 1830s.

This illustration, entitled "Three Delaware Indians," shows chief Bod-a-sin and his wife, Ah-wee, alongside Non-on-day-gon, a famous warrior.

for **muskets** and, by the mid-1700s, they were handling firearms with great skill—particularly long rifles, which they used in hunting and fighting. Lenape warriors were admired for their shooting accuracy, as well as their ability to repair their weapons.

During the 1700s, the Lenape and other tribes living near English settlers moved to Western Pennsylvania and then to Ohio and other parts of the Midwest. Unfortunately, this brought them into contact with the French, England's longtime enemy. War broke out between the two world powers in 1754. Most Lenape warriors fought against the British, who defeated the French, while some fought beside English soldiers. During the American Revolution, most Lenape warriors served

with the colonists against England as scouts and soldiers.

After the United States won its independence, the Lenape became the first Native Americans to sign a treaty with the new nation. But the peace did not hold. As settlers continued to push west, Lenape leaders joined the Northwest Confederacy, a collection of tribes that agreed to fight as one in order to stop the U.S. government from taking more Native land.

Lenape warriors launched deadly raids on American settlers and participated in major battles. In 1791, their great war chief, Buckongahelas, led them to victory over a U.S. military force at the Battle of the Wabash, in Ohio. Lenape warriors, along with their Shawnee and Miami allies, launched a sophisticated attack on more than 1,000 soldiers.

The U.S. soldiers killed by Lenape, Miami, and Shawnee forces during the Battle of the Wabash represented around a quarter of the nation's army at the time. Only a handful survived. To this day, it is still the worst defeat in American history.

◀ Lenape warriors were feared hand-to-hand fighters.

# A NEW REALITY

The **Northwest Indian War** ended in 1794, following a defeat at the Battle of Fallen Timbers. The Lenape signed the Treaty of Greenville, which promised they would never fight against the United States again. Their people scattered after that, with most moving to Indiana, then Kansas, and finally to Oklahoma beginning in the late 1850s. Some settled in Missouri, others in Wisconsin. One group received a **land grant** from Spain in 1820 and moved to East Texas—but American settlers later drove them off their lands. Others left America entirely, migrating north to Canada.

Individual populations of Lenape and Delaware people were very small. As a result, they sometimes found it advantageous to align themselves with larger, more powerful tribes. For example, in 1867, the Lenape purchased land in Oklahoma from the Cherokees. They believed they would become citizens of the Cherokee Nation, but that did not turn out to be the case.

This painting shows the Treaty of Greenville. The Lenape promised never to fight against the U.S. government again.

Starting in the 1930s, Lenape tribal members experienced a reawakening of their identity. Over the next 90 years, several lawsuits and legal cases led to official recognition of three groups: the Delaware Nation and the Delaware Tribe of Indians—both located in Oklahoma—and the Stockbridge-Munsee Community, in Wisconsin. Thousands of people of Lenape heritage live elsewhere in the U.S. and Canada (where reservations are called "reserves"). There are two reserves in the province of Ontario: the Munsee-Delaware Nation and the Delaware Nation of Moraviatown. These populations have called Canada home since the late 1700s.

# BEING LENAPE

Before the arrival of European settlers, the Lenape people were similar to most **Eastern Woodland** tribes. They hunted a wide range of animals, including deer, elk, black bears, rabbits, turkeys, geese, and beavers. They took advantage of fish and other resources from the two major rivers in their territory, as well as the Atlantic Ocean. They also benefitted from farming the region's rich soil. Like many Native Americans, they raised corn, beans, and squash. These plants—called the "Three Sisters"—grow together and offer a **complete protein**.

The Lenape were a highly mobile people. They used the many waterways in their territory like roads and highways.

This illustration shows a Delaware family from the 1600s.

This recreation of a Lenape wigwam shows how the tribe lived when Europeans first encountered them.

They built dugout canoes made by hollowing out tree trunks. The tulip tree was their favorite, but they also worked with elm, oak, and chestnut. The canoes used by tribes to the north, such as the Iroquois, were lighter and more maneuverable because they were made from birch bark. The bark from the birch trees that grew on Lenape lands was not suitable for canoe-making.

Women's duties in the Lenape culture typically included planting and harvesting, gathering wild plants for food and medicine, and making and repairing

▲
Lenape clans were based on a mother's kinship.

clothing. Men in the tribe handled hunting, village defense, and heavy chores—including the building of their living structures. Most Lenape lived in domed huts called wigwams, which were made from young trees joined together and covered with bark or animal hides. In some cases, larger structures called longhouses were built. They could hold several members of the same family or **clan**.

The Lenape people were bound together by their three main clans: Turkey, Wolf, and Turtle. If a mother belonged to one clan, then her children would belong to that same clan too. Clans were based on a mother's kinship, so women had considerable influence and were involved in almost every major decision.

Marriage among clan members was forbidden, so the relationships between different clans within the same community—as well as relationships between the Unalachtigo, Munsee, and Unami groups—were vast and complex. The Turkey clan was closely associated with the Unalachtigo, who lived in southern New Jersey and Delaware, and whose name meant "people who live by the ocean." The Wolf clan was associated with the Munsee, who lived in northern New Jersey and southern New York. Their name meant "people of the stone country." The Turtle clan provided leadership to the Unamis, who lived in central and western New Jersey and along the Delaware River in Pennsylvania. Their name meant "people who live downriver."

No women are believed to have been involved in the 1626 transaction with the Dutch for Manhattan. So did the Munsee men have the authority to make this deal? It is an interesting question!

# SOMETHING SACRED

The Lenape people feel a deep connection to the natural and spirit world. This is reflected in their origin story. They believe in a supreme being named Kishelemakank, who created the Earth after dreaming of mountains, rivers, forests, animals, and people. A giant turtle rose from the ocean, its shell becoming the land. A tree grew on this shell and, from that tree, the first man and woman were created. Kishelemakank also made the sun, moon, and seasons.

The stories and legends Lenape parents told their children featured the animals they encountered in their environment. They included deer, rabbits, foxes, raccoons, squirrels, and owls. These animals had human qualities that helped young people see that they were connected to everything in nature.

For this reason, the concept of land ownership did not fit neatly into the Lenape belief system. Land was something to be used and shared—and sometimes fought over—but not something that could be traded or

This 1921 painting shows a spiritual celebration in Oklahoma. Ceremonial life has played an important role in Lenape culture wherever they have lived.

sold. This put them at a disadvantage in their dealings with European settlers. In the late 1800s, when the United States government passed a law that reservation land had to be divided into individual **parcels**, it was extremely disruptive to Lenape culture.

Holding on to cultural traditions and values has often been challenging for the Lenape people. Responsibility for keeping these traditions alive falls to tribal elders and creative people within the Lenape community. One way they maintain this connection is through their art, which is deeply influenced by their respect for nature and links to their ancestors. Lenape

basketry, **gourd** art, and beadwork feature traditional designs. For many centuries, the Lenape were known for the magnificent shoulder bags (also known as **bandoliers**) used by their hunters and warriors.

Joe Baker is an artist and educator who traces his ancestry back to the tribal leader that made the first treaty with William Penn. He has devoted much of his life to keeping cultural traditions alive. Recently, he recreated a Lenape bandolier for an exhibit at the Metropolitan Museum of Art in New York City.

In addition to teaching at Columbia University in New York, Baker was appointed to the board of the New York Foundation for the Arts in 2022. He has worked as executive director of Lenape Center partnerships with prestigious organizations, including the Brooklyn Museum of Art, American Ballet Theater, and the Whitney Museum of Art.

"I felt a certain sense of loss for this important cultural article of dress," Joe Baker explains. "I wanted to, if possible, teach myself how to make one through hands-on study of actual historic bags. My hope was to bring this art form back to our people in our community."

◀ Displaying traditional arts and crafts at festivals has helped to introduce the public to Lenape culture.

# PAST, PRESENT, FUTURE

More than 16,000 people in the United States trace their heritage to Lenape ancestors; around 2,500 more live in Canada. All identify themselves as either Delaware, Lenape, or Lenni Lenape. Though separated by great distance, they are connected by their culture through shared celebrations and ceremonies, as well as annual gatherings. The internet has proved especially valuable for strengthening the bonds between different communities—and also sharing Lenape stories, songs, art, and other important traditions.

For more than a century, the economy on the reservations in Oklahoma and Wisconsin where the Lenape people lived was very **depressed**. In 1988, the United States government passed the Indian Gaming Regulatory Act, which allowed tribes to operate casinos on reservation lands. The Stockbridge-Munsee people operate the North Star Mohican Casino Resort, while the Delaware Nation in Oklahoma operates the Gold River

The Lenape people have advocated for fair treatment for generations. This photo shows a group of tribal leaders who traveled to Washington, D.C., in 1866.

Casino. These businesses have provided a critical boost to the Lenape economy.

One of the greatest threats to Native American culture is the loss of a tribe's language. Centuries of warfare, disease, and forced relocation greatly reduces tribal populations—which reduces the number of people who keep the old words alive. In the 1980s, only a handful of fluent speakers of the Lenape language were still living. Fortunately, hard work began on a project that would

become the Lenape Talking Dictionary in 2002. It has since grown to more than 15,000 words.

In 2022, the Brooklyn Public Library in New York created an exhibition that honored this important effort. It brought together Lenape people who live on the federally recognized reservations in Oklahoma and Wisconsin, and on the reserve in Ontario, Canada—and also included tribe members who live in traditional Lenape areas in New Jersey, Delaware, and Pennsylvania.

These groups make efforts to protect the Lenape culture in various ways, including attempts to reclaim land through the legal system. In 2002, the Lenape Nation of Pennsylvania sued the government for some of the land lost in the notorious 1737 Walking

◀ Three Lenape men pose for a photo during a Native American cultural event. Efforts to preserve the Lenape language have met with great success over the last 25 years.

Purchase, but was unsuccessful. In 2019, the Ramapough Lenape Nation in northern New Jersey regained the right to use land it owns in the town of Mahwah for ceremonies and cultural events that had taken place there for centuries. Mahwah—the Lenape word for "meeting place"—had tried to restrict these activities with changes in **zoning** and permits.

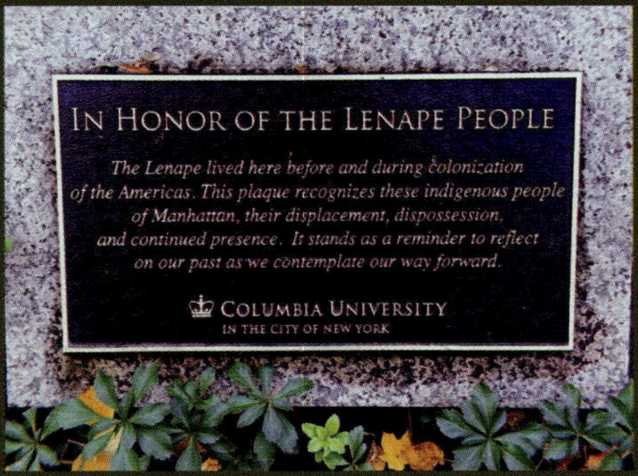


The effort to acknowledge traditional Lenape territory has also enjoyed success in a place many thought would be impossible: the island of Manhattan, one of the five boroughs of New York City. The Dutch "purchased" Manhattan from the Munsee people in 1626 and the **state seal** of New York includes an image of a Lenape man. In 2016, Columbia University dedicated a plaque on its campus in honor of the Lenape people. It recognizes that the Lenape lived there before the colonization of America and acknowledges their **dispossession** and displacement.

◀ Celebrations of Lenape life and traditions are crucial to protecting the tribe's heritage and culture.

# GLOSSARY AND FURTHER READING

## GLOSSARY

**Abundant**—Offering plenty of food.

**Algonquian**—A family of Indigenous languages originating from the Atlantic and Great Lakes regions.

**Bandolier**—A type of shoulder belt.

**Clan**— A close-knit extended family related by kinship or common ancestors.

**Commerce**—The activity of buying, selling, and trading.

**Complete Protein**— A protein that contains all nine amino acids the human body needs.

**Depressed**—Suffering from a lack of demand and employment.

**Dialect**—A slightly different form of a language spoken by people in specific areas.

**Dispossession**—Depriving people of their land or property.

**Domain**—An area controlled by a group of people or government.

**Eastern Woodland**—An area in the eastern United States and southeastern Canada that is used to describe Indigenous people and their cultures.

**Gourd**—A large fruit with hard skin.

**Land Grant**—A gift of real estate or territory by a government.

**Muskets**—Long guns fired once before reloading through the muzzle, which were commonly used until the late 1800s.

**Northwest Indian War**—A conflict between the U.S. government and a confederacy of Native Americans in the late 1700s for control of the current-day states of Ohio, Indiana, Michigan, Illinois, and Wisconsin.

**Parcels**—Units of land that can be bought and sold.

**State Seal**—A symbol of a state's identity, used on official documents.

**Wrested**—Took through force or intimidation.

**Zoning**—Local laws that govern how property can and cannot be used.

## BOOKS


Krupat, Arnold. *Boarding School Voices: Carlisle Indian School Students Speak*. Lincoln, NE: University of Nebraska Press, 2021.

Rossiter, Brienna. *The Trail of Tears*. Mendota Heights, MN: North Star Editions, 2025.

Tyler, Ron. *Native Americans: The Complete Plates of McKenney, Catlin, and Bodmer*. Cologne, Germany: Taschen America, 2024.

Various Authors. *My Life: Growing Up Native in America*. New York, NY: MTV Books/Simon & Schuster Children's Publishing, 2024.


## ABOUT THE AUTHOR

**MARK STEWART** has written more than 150 non-fiction books for educational publishers, covering history, sports, and popular culture. His family tree tells a complex story common to many Americans. Mark's ancestors include some of the first European colonists, as well as the Indigenous people with whom early settlers interacted. Some faced off on the field of battle while others fought side-by-side. His 10th great-grandfather was **Myles Standish**, an officer on the ***Mayflower***, while his ninth great-grandmother was **Singing Bird Corbison**, who was described as a "Shawnee woman" but who was probably from the **Wampanoag** tribe. The Wampanoag people saved Standish and his fellow **Pilgrims** from starvation during the winter of 1620–21, forming the basis for the story of Thanksgiving. The descendants of Corbison and Standish blended into a single family in 1789, and then headed west in search of opportunity. This brought Mark's ancestors into direct conflict with Native people along the frontier in the 1700s and 1800s. Mark's sixth great-grandmother recalled frantically casting bullets for her husband as they defended their small Kentucky fort from an attack. Another served under 23-year-old **Abraham Lincoln** in the Illinois Militia during the Black Hawk War of 1832. Mark's more recent ancestors chose to fight their battles with words—as writers and editors of books, newspapers, and magazines. In 2007, he authored a history of the **Indian Removal Act of 1830** and the infamous **Trail of Tears**.

# INDEX